# Chaos Calls

## Julie McNamara

Publication Data

Published in 2012
by
Vital Xposure
People Show Studios
Pollard Row
London E2 6NB

company limited by guarantee
registered in England & Wales
No. 7488858

Poems & illustrations © 2012 Julie McNamara

Edited by Joe Bidder and Hilary Porter
Cover design by Lesley Willis
Back cover portrait © Caglar Kimyoncu

ISBN 978-0-9571851-0-4

British Library Cataloguing-in-Publication data.
A catalogue record for this book is available
from The British Library

Typeset by Hilary Porter and Lesley Willis
and printed in Great Britain by
Antony Rowe, Chippenham, Wiltshire

# Prior Publications

'Madinah' previously published in 'Under The Asylum Tree' Survivors' Press ©1994

'Grief', 'She', 'The Prozac Princess' previously published in: 'Fresher Than Green, Brighter Than Orange' Survivors' Press ©1998

'Holton Haiku' commissioned by Holton Lee © 2001

'Millbank' and 'A Thought For His Mother' commissioned by ICI ©2003

'The Night Before Release' published in 'We Have Come Through' Bloodaxe Books ©2003

'Chaos Calls', 'Eulogy For My Father', 'd'Anu', 'Plastic Paddies', 'Wind' originally published as 'Morning Wind', 'We'll Come To Power' previously published in: 'Irish Lifelines' Irish Women Survivors in London' ©2008 London Irish Women's Centre

'Chaos Calls', 'Prozac Princess', 'The Night Before Release' also published in 'Telling Stories' Karnac Books ©2010

# Acknowledgements

Thanks to Joe Bidder and Hilary Porter for their endless enthusiasm, painstaking editing and encouragement.

to Lesley Willis whose commitment and passion remained steadfast throughout.

to Madinah Fatima Miriam Usman who has rarely failed me.

to Jo Broadwood, Caglar Kimyoncu, Amantha Murphy, Maire Clerkin, Maria Robinson, David Roche, Joe McConnell, Marie Mulholland and to all my dearest friends who held me through the dark.

to my Bobby Browne Sisters, Bernie de Lord and Hetty May Bailey for endless love and laughter.

to my Nan Greta Minto, whose stories kept me going.

to my family in all your gory glory. May love and laughter fill your hearts.

to hope ...

# Foreword

Too many deaths too close to me left me mad with grief. Then I felt I would never breathe easy again. Crisp white sheets and long cold corridors seemed easier than the visceral pain of loss. It was the random senselessness of it all that nearly broke me.

Chaos became my home.

And writing through the chaos wreaked by the great void in my heart kept me alive. I now offer you a glimpse of the first faltering steps towards hope, the breath of life again.

# Index

## It's Cold Out There

| | |
|---|---|
| A Solitary Date | 1 |
| Greenham | 2 |
| Hollywood Parade | 3 |
| Holton Haiku | 4 |
| Learning Curve | 5 |
| Millbank | 6 |
| Plastic Paddies | 7 |
| Misery Gnaws | 8 |
| We'll Come To Power | 9 |
| Thank You For The Flowers | 10 |
| A Thought For His Mother | 12 |

## The Journey

| | |
|---|---|
| Valley Of The Shadows | 17 |
| Chaos Calls | 18 |
| The Prozac Princess | 20 |
| Grief | 21 |
| Place Of Safety Orders | 22 |
| The Hag o' Bheara | 24 |
| Abandon Hope | 26 |
| Iguana Dance | 27 |
| Hearing Voices | 28 |
| Conscious Coma | 29 |
| The Night Before Release | 30 |
| Dibbuk | 32 |
| d'Anu | 34 |
| Wind | 35 |
| The Elephant Dance | 36 |

## Mother

| | |
|---|---|
| Anal Sacks | 40 |
| A Step Ahead | 41 |
| Mend Me | 42 |
| Silver Shoes | 43 |
| Wandering Alarm | 44 |
| You'd Better Come Home | 45 |
| Your Father | 46 |
| Eulogy For My Father | 47 |

## Love

| | |
|---|---|
| Mae | 51 |
| She | 52 |
| I Look Like Daddy | 53 |
| She Prefers Blood | 54 |
| Hot Havana | 55 |
| Letting Go | 56 |
| Madinah | 57 |

## Illustrations

| | |
|---|---|
| Freight Train | 1 |
| Daddy's Home | 11 |
| Place Of Safety | 14 |
| Cliffhanger | 16 |
| Specimen | 23 |
| Angel Of Death | 33 |
| Clearing | 38 |
| Lost | 48 |
| Dervish | 50 |
| Thy Will Be Done | 58 |

# It's Cold Out There

## A Solitary Date

Before bulimia hit the headlines
courtesy of our Queen
and the dysfunctional family of our era
hit my T.V. screen
I thought I was outside it all
an on-looker to the fray
but now we market madness
so I'll be famous for a day.
I'm just another nobody
a kind of mediocre madwoman
as loveless as Lady Di
but without her kind of pay.
If my ansaphone tapes
had been swiped and swept
across those media moguls' magazines
I might have won a prize
but a solitary date
for a smear test
doesn't make much reading
of one's social diary

# Greenham

It's twenty years since I walked here
the battlements had to fall
Thatcher likened Greenham's fence
to the fierce Berlin wall

Oh, I never thought to see the day
when peals of laughter filled
these empty nuclear bases
on Greenham's gentle hills

Creative inspiration!
spread your colours on these walls
where once weapons of destruction
stockpiled within these very halls

Observe how the heart beats now
the passion that baits our breath
art from the heart moved from mind's eye
has replaced the stench of death

## Hollywood Parade

I'm gazing up the boulevard
the pretty prisons built on high
where precious souls in gated homes
sit in ivory towers to the sky

A whole new breed of human
wind tunnels forced the face
frozen features front the fraud
stretched forever into place

and I feel unreal outside it all
it's itching at my skin
seeping through my watery veins
let the Truman Show begin

I swear a pledge to gravity
I'm returning to the soil
it's a bit by bit retrieval
of Mother Nature's toil

I'll raise a glass on parting
praise how far I've come
the errant pathways trodden
against a setting sun

In praise of every wrinkle
the maps of love and life
lines enshrined in humble flesh
unfit for LA life

# Holton Haiku

Gathered there that night
the would-be celebrants
searching for new moons

we exchanged stories
elders of Aquarius
picking out the path

some hailed past poets
more railed lost heroes now gone
their work still leads us

deer tracks carve old grooves
disability's new shoes
though we party on

the land yields promise
its' secrets lure successes
invokes our magic

absent Black comrades
still say we missed the point
yet we are searching

we have travelled far
inclusion, integration
new tunes for old songs

## Learning Curve

We've barred him for being a bully
well he's clearly out of control
it really doesn't matter to us
that he's only four years old

We've alerted social services
surely he's at risk at home
see his mother's a single parent
you know, raising the child alone

No. We didn't think to let her know
or seek her comments at all
the paperwork still has to be done
statistics, targets, shortfall

Yes. I know he's an infant with issues,
I'm aware that he's not quite four
we've had to move fast to statement him
and get him out that door

I'm told his mother is registered blind
but I didn't know when we wrote
why she'd ignored the invitation
and all our other notes...

# Millbank

I remember the Ivory towers
The grandeur and the style
Of those lofty halls of Millbank
In the midst of the Royal mile

Room upon room
Like polished teak tombs
Divided one and all
Devoid of any human touch
The old order had to fall

I remember the splendour
Of the sixth floor view
With a window on the Thames
And that charming chap
Who poled the shagpile
And carefully kissed our hems

But d'you know whilst I remember
That plush carpet on the sixth floor
I cannot recall the name of the man
Who spent seven years opening my door

## Plastic Paddies

Your kind is the worst of all
you're the ones keep brewing trouble
bunch o' bloody blow-ins
Thou shalt not trespass against us

Were you born on the soil?
sure, you wouldn't understand
just like my daughter, my son, my mam
with your romance and reveries
old notions of home...

It wasn't famine forced us out
there was food enough fer you people
you Brits had your eye on all the best land
we'd to leave Ireland to survive

My children are English, born and bred for the Queen
we all celebrate St Patrick's,
long for bacon and cabbage
an' dance a reel or a jig to put Flatley to shame

We laugh about Liverpool, first port of call
where they fleeced us for fares to brave new lands
capital of Ireland, two cathedrals
and left us spent at the bars

You're caught between the devil
and the deep grey blow-in sea
not here nor there
a long way from Clare and even farther from Tralee

"Nick nack paddy whack give a dog a bone
all you Paddies piss off home..."

# Misery Gnaws

Misery gnaws her
Five strong sons all dead and gone
Sarajevo burns

Her face beautiful creases
Scarf a voluptuous frame
Eighty years of grief

Three generations
Shrink back from the brink of hell
She lights the peace flame

Dark weathered fingers
On her finely chiselled hands
Who'd have thought she'd kill?

## We'll Come To Power

We'll come to power in the ageing dance
in our awkward gait with life's romance

we'll come to power in our ecstasy
when we give up courting agony

we'll come to power when you least expect
distracted by coded intellect

we'll come to power as celebrants
we'll rock and reel in our own sweet chants

we'll come to power we wise we small
weakened by warring wee sufferers all

we'll come to power and the world shall heal
when the bureaucrats have learned to feel

we'll come to power the tragic, the brave
ranting and wheeling on your grave

# Thank You For The Flowers

Thank you for the flowers
your condolences and tears
thank you for the awkward smiles
embarrassed silences
your fear

Thank you for the limelight
the place in the front pew
the quickly bought Mass cards
you recognise the fact
that we were Lovers
though never joined in church

Candle-lit forgiveness
shines a light into our world
at last you know
although you'd rather not
that we knew each other
biblically
I watch your awkward crooked faces
display your awkward crooked hearts

We were never as we should have been
inside your tightly-knitted robes
your stereotypes steep pain
and stifle passion
your words wound

And yet we danced
we kissed
and wrapped our legs around each other
exultant in our passionate display
rampant in our love of life and of each other

but all you saw was shame
dirty sheets
and empty christening gowns
in barren cribs.

## A Thought For His Mother...

His Mother says he was a fine young man
her only son
a man of gentleness and integrity
who dreamed of a better world
of brave new horizons
at the expense of body mind and soul

It is *not* that the giddy heights of
targets soaring
onwards and ever upwards
or the bigger better bartering in industry
eats away at life
just that *his* light was spent too soon
a lesson in careful budgeting

Our financial analysts
wait nervously
under scrutiny of the local paparazzi
how will the land lie
when we have buried our dead?
The edges of the carpet have grown thick
fat with the remnants of old yarns
shovelled in furtive corners

It is not the failed imagination
but the cold betrayal of trust
in your leadership
in the spirit of team enterprise
that leaves her sore with grief
sales are sinking fast
with every Mother's heart

Value for each shareholder
may mean more than money
we sweat and serve
pushing those who serve us
until push comes to shove
accidents will happen...

It is not that the industry
so carelessly discards
its human cargo
but he was unique
certainly one of few statistics
put it down
to natural wastage

Where does it say in our Mission Statement
that we can disregard his life
disrespect
disown him
belittle and abuse him
as an irritating flaw
in an otherwise
perfect
learning curve?

Our reputation
in the wilderness
reduced
as we reduced this man
to misery
with a slip of the pen
does the ethos of our company
so little value life?

They liked you in the papers Sir
until the case last year
you wriggled under crossfire
and were proved wanting...
pride of place
a private space
in residential care
is not what his Mother had foreseen

# The Journey

# The Valley Of The Shadows

Yea though I walk
through the valley of the shadows
where death has no dominion
I shall fear no evil
and yet I do.
I fear the wretched emptiness
the nothingness that the absence of you
now brings.
I fear the shadows that ape my gait
hugging my frame
that mock and mirror me as I make
another slow stroll home.
I wonder at the dark
the gaping wound
that losing you now wields,
I am lost without your breath
and my very soul is stretched across
the cold clay soil
that snatched you from my breast.

## Chaos Calls

Once in search of stillness
at the eye of the storm
I strode out into the darkest night
to find the water's edge
yearning for belonging
she-son
'Son of the sea hound'
Mac Connemara
shrinking from the earth's surface
and scattering bright electric charges
out into the universe
I stood beneath
the pink imploding stars
chaos called me in

Exhilarated by the storm
my arms outstretched
me the martyr gathering in the stars
I let the rain batter my bones
till my goose-skin flesh
bruised blue with cold
drawn into the raging of the night
and still so out of touch
with chaos incarnate
I flew
over the cliff edge
and closing my eyes
let go one final scream
into the thunderous clouds...

Chaos tantalises
with that lingering
taste of the taboo
riding the storm without a bridle

fucking the Pope without a condom
performing the stations of the cross
in the shape of a clitoris
Mary's
calls me home
chaos is mine...chaos calls me in

They struggled hauling me
up the mud-sodden sheer cliffside
from the precarious ledge
twelve feet below
the rain softer now
I was lost beneath the greyness
of a drab sky drained of drama
lost and yet alert
to new agonies
my heart ached
fresh grazes scorched
as I was yanked crudely
back into the chaos of the day

There are times when
I still dance
with danger as my darling
when suicidal sirens
seduce me to the abandoned abyss
still home inside my heart
but I have learned to surf
to rock an' roll
across the turf
to spit and scream
mad banshee at the shebeen
I have learned to ceoin
when chaos calls me in
when chaos calls me in

## The Prozac Princess

They've worried my mind till I'm weary
drowned me in drugs to despair
yes I'm in the caring circus
with the services who care

Watch me soft-shoe shuffle
on the Diazepam dazzle-dance daze
where all the world's a forget-me-fog
and my whole life's just a phase

Just call me the Prozac Princess
while I rattle round and round
on the magical medical mystery tour
I'm on the miracle cure they've found

They tell me I'll feel much better
Dothiepin's the dope
Britain's sunshine smarty
the quack quack quack's new hope

But you can't bomb me into oblivion
or bleed these brain cells dry
'cause this zombie's into rebellion
this baby's gonna fly

So I've flushed the phenos down the toilet
gave the diazepam to the dog
buried the barbiturates in the garden
I'm going to get myself a job

(I think I'll be a chemist)

## Grief

I can't go on these weary days
in bed with death
with ashes in my mouth

for I have eaten grief wholemeal
and where she gnaws
gentleness will pay

my heart is clouded from the sun
and with each breath I rue the day
mesmerised by the pain
of sudden partings

where carrion flesh buries deep
the joy I seek
I can't go on and on this weary way
for grief will eat me clean away

## Place Of Safety Orders

Oh I little dreamed
when you spoke of safety
and a place where I would be
looked after
that your vision could be
so far from mine.
Were you surprised when ringing for the force
that so many would jump to your service
to cramp in this dance with danger?
Did the image of these handcuffs
clamped behind my back
or those raw restraints
locking my bleeding ankles tight together
shock you too?
Or did the mark
of that great jackboot
stamped across my purple bruised abused body
bear the rubber stamp of your approval?

# The Hag o' Bheara

This auld Scrag
this bitter twisted twig
with snarled and gnarled gut
keeps a cutlass
ever ready in her fist

For the watchful child
rocked and crooned
in tune with terror
war has its kicks
these hard hands fought well
me in ankle shackles
dainty bracelets at my cuffs
spewing foam

Oh I have courted danger at my table
and played the ace of spades
still trussed and wildly splayed
some sad carcass
spent and disarrayed
a dispassionate display

Six broad boots upon my back
whilst they fought to
pin their tails upon this donkey
and dance the devil's jig

I lay beneath the heavens
bejewelled with bracelets
a mockery of our wedding bed
did you know your arse
doesn't open like your cunt
unless your raw arse rips
in giving birth to venom?

There is no stallion can break me in
no horse I have not ridden into hell
no careful ringing of the death knell
whilst I am strung so high

Well tuned to the predator
my body weeps an open wound
seeping through the carapace
that once festered between my thighs

But at midnight's witching hour I howl
the banshee ceoins the cawl
that lures the Scrags to muster
six sons of Hades sent to hell
this auld Scrag
this bitter twisted twig
ever ready
serenades the Sirens at her heart

## Abandon Hope

Abandon hope all ye who enter here
did they mean the womb
the world
or just this grimy cell?
Cold stone concrete
blue blanket
standard issue
badly in need of darning
I don't sew
that smell of piss once more
not mine
one small opening
six small bars
wrought iron
too high
too tired
a bell on the right
'Know a many, trust a few,
learn to paddle your own canoe'
I'm allowed a phone call
I tell the rookie
with easy grin and hard haircut
hates his mother
doesn't do know-alls
decides I'm it
the hatch slams shut

## Iguana Dance

Yesterday
I fell in love
with an Igu-anny-ana
she had a kind of haughty stance
a poise
a pride
magnificence
that lured me to her drama
vivid green
as the lush fan palms
swaying to the gentle dance
of the Iguana's steady charms
pouncing with its sturdy arms
on an innocent tomata

...I wish I was red

## Hearing Voices

I hear voices
Should I see somebody about that?
Shame about these stitches
some of 'em just don't care.
I am still here somewhere
although you may never know
hearing is the last to leave you.
Will you place the lumps
in carefully sorted jam jars?
In formaldehyde?
With clever little labels?
Or dash them in the bin
in disgrace?
But the nurses are on fine form.
You trying again then?
The sooner the better.
God look at these scars!
I don't think you can call yourself a woman
until you're a mother

## Conscious Coma

'Take her to the theatre'
I hear voices through the fog
but cannot find the script,
over and over I search for words
through the luggage of my mind
and yet don't recall the play
that has me lying comatose before you.
Deep inside the cavities of this flesh
I am still here
loitering with intent
though mute
at war within these walls.
My captor wields a scalpel
carefully carves
a continent from my breasts.
I am convinced he had a friend.

They spoke of cricket as I slipped
beyond the veil.
One worked from right to left
with careful stitches pulling me back to life.
And he who worked from left to right
pulled tight, too taut the line,
creating ruched ripples in my skin
says he prefers to work on hands.

## The Night Before Release

*I will put in my case* the ready laugh
that bubbles from a lover's smile ...
*I will put in my case* the drowsy dawn
of a virgin sunrise
*I will put in my case* a bladdered newt
with its tiny glass of Ouzo
*I will put in my case* a tidy row of hard-clogged
centipedes Morris dancing all their way to hell
*I will put in my case* the rich brown, brandied
voice of Billie Holiday
with a tender hand to comfort her when the pain
just won't be soothed
*I will put in my case* the acid tang of sherbet dab
and spanish in its old yellow tube
with bright red writing on
*I will put in my case* old Armitage Shanks
for I have read his name in writing
on many an ill-spent day
*I will put in my case* the beautiful ebony woman
with the easy laugh and wide-boned gait
who scrubs at the hospital, clearing off
the vulnerable remnants
from the porcelain of cabbages and kings
*I will put in my case* the tender love of all my friends
who hold me in their hearts
*I will put in my case* the shrivelled ancient skin
of my embittered grandmother whose leathery
carcase must be fitting for a purse
*I will put in my case* my passion for the mighty sea
whose majesty has called me more than once
to take the plunge and rise again

*I will put in my case* the first tot of Bushmills 17
on a brutal weathered night in Donegal
*I will put in my case* the mischief and smile
of my oldest comrade and Seannachie, Packie Manus
Byrne, and each time I dare to lift the lid
I'll hear him cry: Auch!
Never let the truth get in the way of a good story!
*I will put in my case* the magic of dragons that fly,
the violent blue of kingfishers
*I will put in my now very large case* a fine display
of rubber penises of every height and hue, a pair
of jellied eels with KY tubes and rubber lube
*I will put in my case* a snugly fitting pair of snappy
yellow marigolds and a squeaky leather cane
*I will put in my case* a dose of salts for Lot, a pair of
scales for Solomon, a needle and thread
for John the B, an extra rib for Adam,
a pair of specs for Eve (for she surely needed them)
and a special word for Lucifer for he's had
a very bad press!

There's a lot to be said for medication.

# Dibbuk

The Dibbuk's been dancing cheek to cheek
I never feel quite whole
like some sultry-lipped Svengali
this full-bosomed Mata Hari
she's sucking at my soul

I long to be immortal
but that's close to self deceit
the divine don't do depression
not even nervous disposition
on their sunny sunny streets

Dothiepin's my dark red wine
doctor's favourite little tipple
Sertraline's safe for partying
for cosy sunshine smartying
when I really want the nipple

She's still sitting on my shoulder
tap dancing to the blues
as I watch the years grow older
the Dibbuk's getting feistier
in her ruby red clog shoes

Counting up the tiny demons
in their space capsules heading high
the longer that they linger there
swarming through my mist filled air
I know I'll never see the sky

The Dibbuk's lying low today
the devil's headed for the hills
it could be time to breathe
this is D day this is Me day
I've flushed away the pills

## d'Anu

The soft and gentle rains of Erin
fall constantly upon your ancient face
upturned to promises
of sunlight
searing through the gloom
rainbows of every shade and hue
riddle the puddles
of these pock marked streets
on a Kerry afternoon

Nerves snipped at the neck
my head is sorrow worn
hung low and dragging in the sod
Until a trickle of tearful sky
causes me to raise my sights once more
and seeking out the faded arcs of colour
hanging in the clouds
I grasp the message

Hope

is what we do with our despair

# Wind

When the morning wind comes whistling in
its breath combing the trees
I feel the world awake with me
and face the day with ease
I nurse the smell of heaven
in the wildness of these lands
rushing strands of strange new senses
through these heavy hands

When the wind is wild with anger
and raging at these shores
I hold close the stillness of the storm
inside that passionate furore
and feast upon the terror time
the bold strokes in bright array
until the torrent's spent at last
that last gasp ekes away

When the morning wind comes rushing in
and finds me lost in fear
I turn my cheek to feel the pulse
of nature drawing near
and I learn to trust the movement
of the earth beneath my feet
to greet the Thyme with Rosemary
to taste the bittersweet

## The Elephant Dance

On moonlit nights when the silver stars
shimmer with delight
winking at the towns below sleeping out of sight
the lumbering sturdy elephants
make through the trees to join their dance

With wrinkled flesh and baggy knees
they slowly gather in the midnight breeze
and side by side in fine array
the heavy ones begin to sway

Their rumbling pierces the clouds
as the wee ones trumpeting aloud
step inside the gentle trance
of fifty elephants who dance

And to this day we can't know why
they meet to shiver heave and sigh
but the thunder of their wondrous thighs
can move the storms to lullabies

Mesmerising all who feel
vibrations of their Ele-wheel
a circle of earth-bound big-eared beasts
majestic movers to the feast

But when night has flown and day is dawn
the land lies empty and forlorn
they leave no sign there's not a trace
of elephants dancing in that place

While some believers celebrate
historians haggle o'er their fate
and swear they're all quite dead and gone
but their dancing stories linger on

It is said that elephants roaming wild
are witnessed only by a child
who makes up all their Ele-dances
and joins the magic of their trances

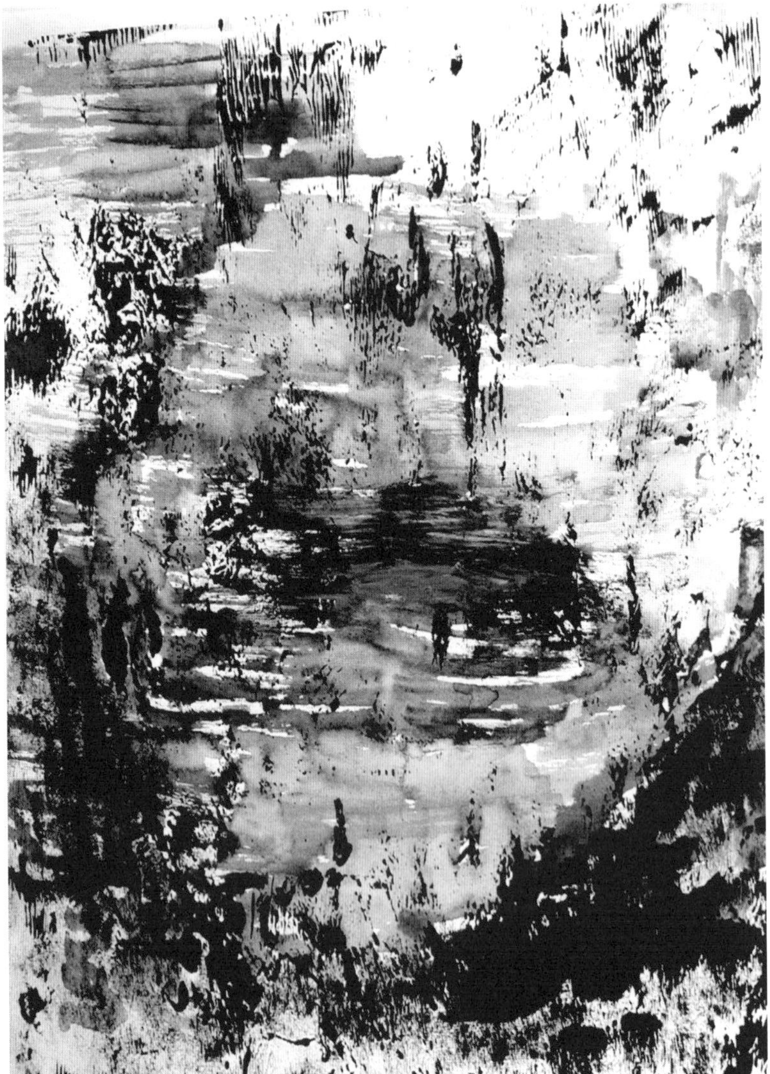

# Mother

## Anal Sacks

I'm not going to that vet again
she announces
clasping her bedraggled belongings
to her heart
unspeakable
what he said he'd do
to my beloved dog
in broad daylight
Anal sacks?
all she needs is worming

## A Step Ahead

I want you to keep a step ahead
you won't let them put me away will you?
They're hastening me to my death
might as well measure me for a shroud
I'd prefer pink
take these papers
make a note of the bank account
she's put her name on it
kept my car and my mobility allowance
picking over my bones
and I'm still using them
tell her, tell them all
she's not having power
of my eternity

## Mend Me

You told me that the skies were filled
with the loving arms of those
we two have lost.
You taught me the secrets
in the cloisters of the church
like the folds of Nan's blue dancing frock
the fraught passions pulled taut
across our father's brow.
You taught me how to fight with pride
now mend my muddied heart
for when I howl at the night skies
my tears wrung from my spleen
and I am broke in two
I expect you there to carry me.
I need you to hold me in your heart still more
now you are gone
for I will not play the martyr
married to death for ever
abandoned here to soldier on.

## Silver Shoes

She sits me down and tells me
with a flush of fresh energy -
I made a plan
I've asked them all to come to my funeral
but I'm not buying all the booze
Danny drinks too much
and I don't like whiskey
I've rung them all
my friends
most of them are dead
well they don't drink
but we'll have a bloody good dance
and I'll wear my favourite shoes
you know the ones
they're glitter grey

# Wandering Alarm

    Bleeeep
*Mrs McNamara, Are you all right?*
    Bleeeep
Who is this?
How did we trigger the alarm?
    Bleeeep
*You have a wandering alarm.*
*Are the doors secured?*
    Bleeeep
This is her daughter
Have you tagged my mother?
    Bleeeep
*Can I speak to Mrs McNamara please?*
Well she's currently wandering with a glass of whisky
I'll see if she'll talk to you
    Bleeeep
Hello, yes?
*What's your name?*
I'm Mrs McNamara
that's my daughter you were talking to
we're having a little drink
    Bleeeep
*That's very good Mrs McNamara.*
*Are you all right?*
    Bleeeep
I'm having a High Commissioner.
Are you a psychiatrist?
*No*
Well I never mix my shrinks
    Bleeeep

## You'd Better Come Home

You'd better come home
I might not be in when you call
they said I might be ill
dementing
I won't know what you look like
any more
I'll miss you when I'm gone
don't be so out of touch...

What's your name again?

## Your Father

She offered
the gravy boat
with jaded sprouts
and cold roast potatoes

Twenty six years to gather this clan
this sham
of a family
built on lies
bellies tense we wait
not for the food
but some crumb of comfort
wisdom from the mountain

Where they have taken my mother
this changeling sits instead
still we wait
for signs of life
some remnant of the love
we never had

'I'd like to say something'
she falters

Open mouthed
we gape
at the gift

'Your father
was a very good fuck you know'

## Eulogy For My Father

Drink was his ruin
Masked his poetry and pain
Thus he hid from life

Songs with aching heart
Pulled taut passions on his brow
Turmoil wants ways out

Old comrades long dead
All drinking for the famine
Peace was a stranger

So shy of laughter
There you'd find him shedding tears
Gave the game away

Though he loved passion
Sparked fires on wet stormy nights
He never learned to swim

He rose with the tide
Paid tribute to Erin's isle
And was dead by dawn

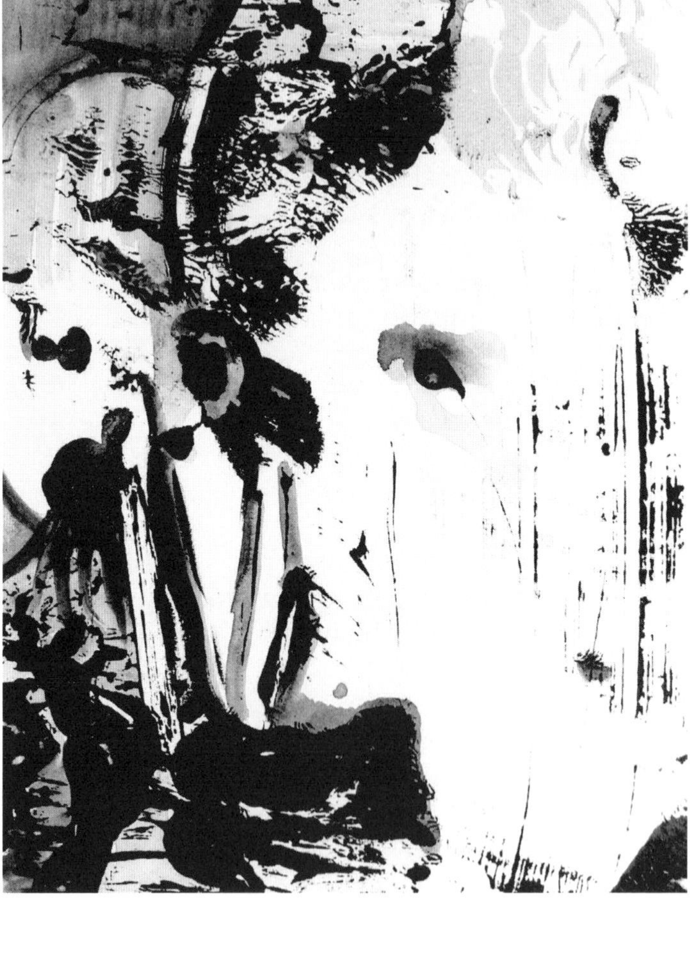

# Love

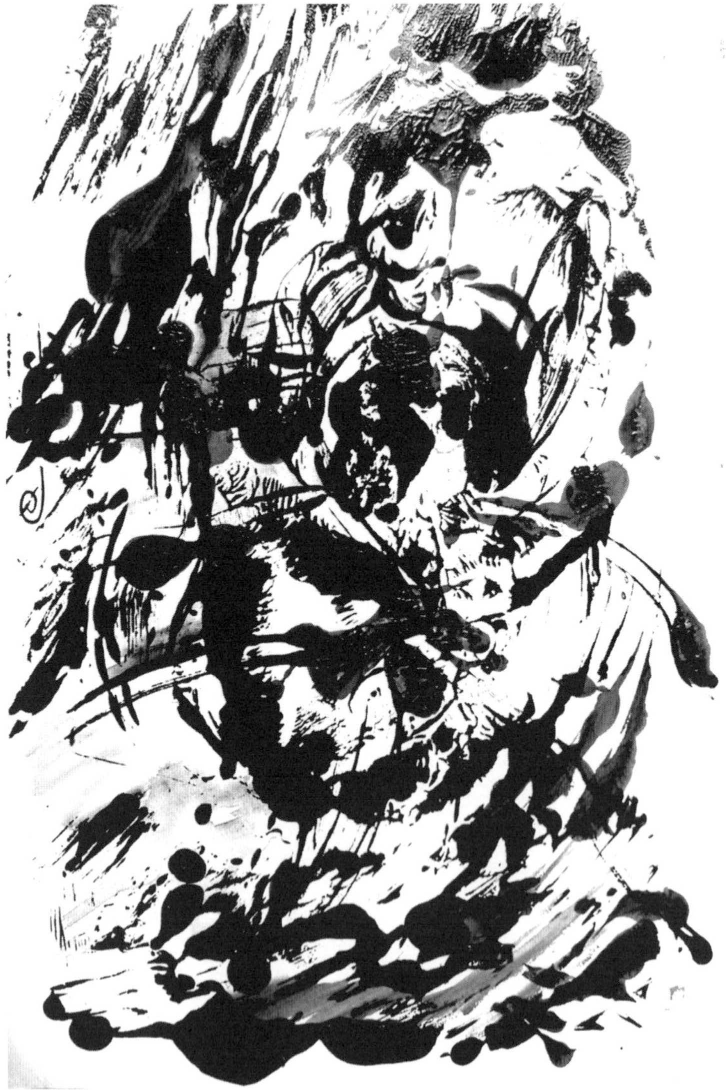

## Mae

In the closing notes
the keys jarred
the pianist hummed a harmony
eyes slow and wistful
and fumbling fingers
plinked
plink-plonked
a sorry little fistful
that worried at the keyboard
crudely s h a t t e r i n g
the pipe dream
      ivory tower
         she had scaled
to play a sad concerto
to the pallid looking dreamer
sat staring seaward
towards the Irish flow
the watery grave
of one who sang that same old song
not so long ago.
She sits beside the piano
above her blousy bosom
fingering a cigarette
scattering ash haphazardly
staring through the smoke-filled
beer-swilled
shebeen
fretting over the fragments
of another
broken dream

# She

she loves fruit
and she's married an onion
she loves a scrap
so she's fighting for peace
and she's always always right

she loves to dance
with dervishes
and deal the upper hand
so she's going East to find herself
to flirt with death and demons

because she loves fruit
and she's married an onion

that's why she left me

## I look Like Daddy

She sits wrapped tightly
around an open wound
sulphating with need
I am sucked in
looking back in anguish
I cannot find the crumbs
left behind
to lead me home
perpetual sucker
rescuing the lost
I didn't realise
she was looking for Daddy
and I look very like him
if you half close your eyes
in the dark

## She Prefers Blood

A red security blanket
she calls Pochohontis
quiets her pain
we sit with the great chasm
gaping
like an open wound between us
I don't suckle
she is yearning
to feed
sometimes Ovaltine will do
tonight she prefers blood

## Hot Havana

Her arms are wrapped about me
here tonight
whilst the fever's laid me low
and her soft breath sighs
nuzzling
murmurs at my neck

She likes strong arms
around her
craves careful hands
at the meeting of her thighs
mine
are quietly insistent

Her gentle heart
beats to the drum
as I curve
and curl into her
uncertain form

Lured from lullabies
to sweat her pulse
we sway
to the stray
Salsa beat below

We grind
she opens
wide wild orchid
draws me in
and further in
pulsing to the piano
a delicate delivery
of long tapered fingers

## Letting Go

You lulled me gently through the night
your solid arms wrapped close
around my failing flesh
and clinging close
we rocked our way
into the storm

In ripples of this
raw aftermath
we watch in awe
as rivulets of hard-spent tears
etch their pained pathways
from the mountains of our misery
to join the salt spray sea

Sadly now
I watch you go
no more rooted
in darkness
and as I let you go
my love loosens the knotted gut
that anchored
you to me
and we spread our mighty branches
out into the clean air

We
who walked together
warmed each other
through the winters
of the world
have touched each other's soul
and with steady lover's looks
you have smiled into my heart

## Madinah

I saw
eyes bright and shining
a vital love and laughter
in the secrets of your smile
a hidden gleam
that blood red stream
bursting from your soul

I saw
tears upon tears
welling from the deep
resounding echoes
in the silence
hugging at your heart
and a child
grown old with grief
force-fed misery and pain

I saw the harvest apples
manna from heaven
ravaged windfalls
free for all
grown rotten on the ground

Well when you're ready
rotting apples grow the richer
make the sweetest cider
and I'll be sat beside you
while we drink to friendship
and nurse old wounds
forever home!

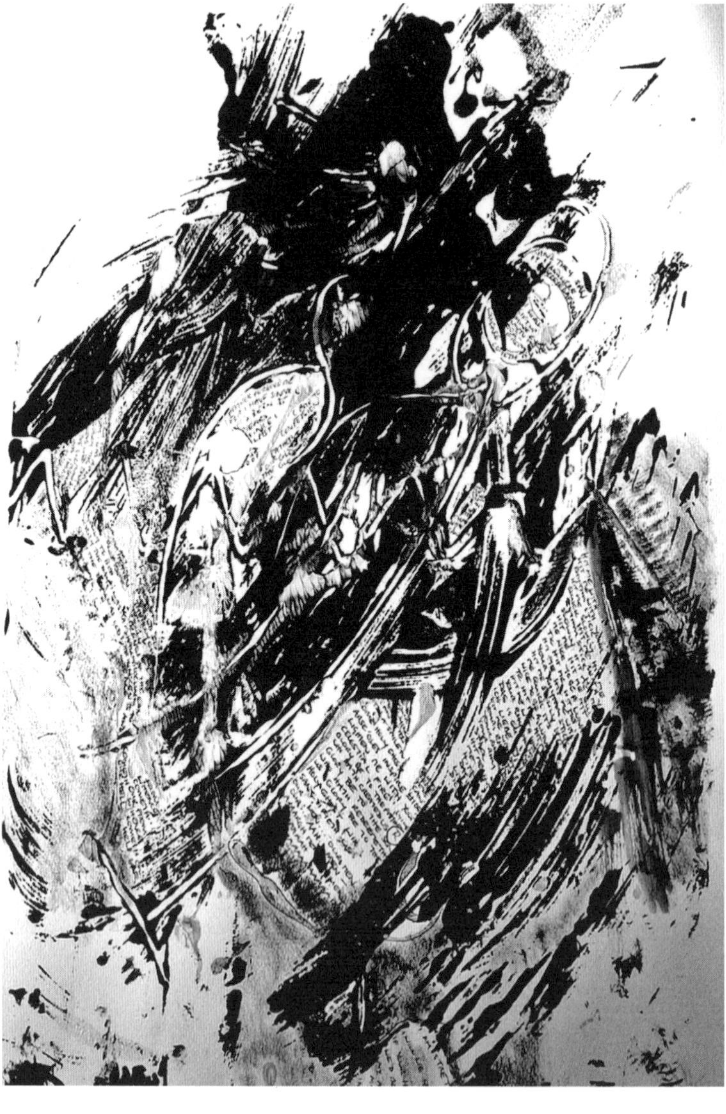